I0164891

A Gift For

From

Always Remember The Final Step

Always Remember...
The Final Step

Always Remember...

The Final Step

Congratulations on beginning your journey!
Dream big as you discover your personal path!

Judy Risner

Copyright © 2009 by Judy Risner

Contributing Editor; Rebecca D. Brown

ISBN 978-0-615-54791-6

Dedication

To Don, my husband and soul mate, for always supporting me while I follow my dreams.   To my children, Jordan and Daryn, and Son in Law, Trent; may you always use God's gifts to reach your true potential as you follow your dreams.

Acknowledgments

I would like to thank my dear friends, Dr. Carl Schreiner and Dr. Terry Schreiner, for taking a chance on me over 30 years ago and for helping me realize my true potential.

I would also like to acknowledge Alan Cohen who gave me the courage to publish this book through reading his inspirational messages in one of his books, "A Deep Breath of LIFE." Thank you to Drs. John and Cathy Jameson for the gift of this book.

Contents

Introduction

Follow your dreams and never give up. You can accomplish anything you want as long as you follow your passion, are willing to work hard, and pray for guidance.

Continue to be proactive about setting goals for what you want in life. While we are not always in control of the things that happen in our lives, we can be in control of how we respond to any challenges.

Included in this book are valuable tools that can help you accomplish your goals, solve problems, and make decisions. You can choose to use these tools to help you turn your dreams into reality.

And always remember the final step...say your prayers and ask for guidance.

Setting Goals

Making your dreams come true.

I truly believe that there is a plan for all of us. Many of us go through each day thinking and dreaming about the future. We dream about what we want to accomplish in our careers, as well as our personal lives. Have you ever had a dream of accomplishing something that seemed out of reach?

I have always been a list writer and have found it helpful to make lists for everything from what needed to be picked up at the grocery store to what my next goals in life would be. When I decided to go to dental hygiene school, I began by making a list of what I needed to do to be able to apply to the program. Then, as each step was completed, I would mark it off my list.

While in college, I began learning more about goal setting. You can compare "goal setting" to "list making" in some ways. The benefit of goal setting is that it helps you accomplish bigger, more complex goals or dreams by breaking them down into smaller tasks. It is a tool that you can use to help you focus on making your dreams come true one step at a time.

There are hundreds, possibly thousands, of books on the theory of goal setting. The goal setting theory has been around for a long time and was first introduced by Aristotle and then in the late 1960's by Dr. Edwin Locke. This theory has withstood the test of time and has been proven to be a solid method to help you continue on the path you desire.

Writing your goals is a wonderful tool to use to get your dreams down on paper so you can make them become reality, otherwise they will remain only dreams. Sometimes the dream or goal can seem out of reach when you look at the big picture, and this method will help it seem less daunting. You will find that the goal setting process will help you identify more attainable steps that will lead to accomplishing your overall goal. Following are some of the things that I have learned along the way that have made some of my dreams become a reality and have helped me focus on the direction I needed to take next.

Prioritize goals. You may have more than one goal. It is important to prioritize your goals in the order of how you want to accomplish them. Put them in order of importance. What do you want to accomplish first?

Position yourself toward your goals. Begin by thinking about what you want. Then begin heading in that direction by following the steps of goals setting. *For example, if you want to climb Mt. Everest you might want to start getting into shape…*

Never share your goals with someone that won't support you. You must remain committed to what you want to accomplish. Don't let others take you off your course.

Never give up. Take it one day at a time and ask, "What do I need to do today to follow what is meant for me?" Be patient; it will happen in the right time.

Follow your Passion. What would you like to be doing even if you didn't get paid for it? Listen to what your heart is telling you and pray for guidance.

What is my passion?

Here are the basic steps of goal setting plus the additional step.

1. Write your goal.

2. Write a detailed plan of how you are going to accomplish your goal. Write out the specific steps one by one.

3. Write beside each step the person who is going to be responsible for that step. (Your name may be by all steps.)

4. Assign a time/date deadline by each step. By what date are you going to have that step completed?

5. Re-evaluate. How is your plan working? Do you need to make any changes to the plan above? Re-write the plan as needed following the same steps listed above.

6. Pray. Begin praying for direction as you determine your goals. Then, continue to ask for guidance every step of the way. I have found it is crucial to ask, "Is this the direction in which I need to be headed? If

so, give me strength. If not, detour me in the right direction." Ask for the wisdom to know the difference. (This step is not necessarily included in the steps of goal setting but has been instrumental in my own personal accomplishments.) This step has truly made the difference in my personal life. *Take it one step at a time. You will reach the goals that are meant for you! You just have to ask.*

As I mentioned above, I have learned to ask, "Am I on the right path? If so, give me the courage to move forward and clear any obstacles from my path. If I am not on the right track, throw obstacles in front of me to make it obvious that I need to head in a different direction."

<u>Goal Setting Exercise (Example)</u>

Step 1. Write your goal.
<u>My goal is; I would like to write a book.</u>

Now apply the remaining steps (2-5):

2. Detailed Plan	3. Person responsible	4. Deadline	5. Re-evaluate
Make a list of what I want to include in my book.	Me	Begin today.	
Get up 30 minutes early each day to write down thoughts.	Me	Begin tomorrow	
Organize thoughts in an outline	Me	End of each month	
Add examples & personal stories	Me	By end of each week	
Research self publishing	Me	60 days before book complete	

Step 6 (Additional Step) Ask for guidance- are you on the right track? (Key to my own personal success.)

Start with where "you are at" in life.

Have you ever said to yourself, "If I ever win the lottery I will ____? Or, if I ever have more time I will____?" Start now. Get your game plan together and do something each day that will lead you in the right direction.

Pick one thing. What one thing are you going to focus on to make a positive difference in your life?

Pray first, plan afterwards. Maybe we are planning in one direction and God's will is in another direction.

You now have learned the basic goal setting principals. Put this tool in your toolbox and apply this method to anything you want to accomplish.

Begin a list of the goals you would like to accomplish. Pick one and apply the steps of goal setting using the forms in the back of this book.

_____

_____

_____

_____

_____

_____

_____

_____

_____

_____

Personal Notes

Personal Notes

_____

_____

_____

_____

_____

_____

_____

_____

_____

_____

_____

_____

_____

_____

_____

_____

_____

Problem Solving

Now, let's discuss a second valuable tool that you will find effective if you run across any roadblocks on your path toward accomplishing your goals. There are basic problem solving skills that, when applied, will help overcome barriers.

This method will help you narrow down which option will best solve your problem by being able to brainstorm all solutions and then narrow them down as you review them one at a time.

Following is one of the problem solving skill exercises that will help you in your everyday life.

1. Write down the problem.

2. Write down all possible solutions.

3. Decide on the best solution. Consider the pros and cons of each solution when making this decision.

4. List the steps needed to begin working on the solution. Then put them in order of priority. What needs to be done first?

5. Assign a name of the person responsible by each step.

6. Determine the time/date by when each step is to be completed.

7. Re-Evaluate (Is the solution working?).

Helpful Hints when using the Problem Solving Method:

❖ Do you need to apply the steps of problem solving to your challenge or is there a simple solution?

❖ List all the solutions no matter how silly they may seem. As you think of solutions, write them down quickly.

❖ Begin marking the least favorable solutions off one at a time until you are left with the best solution.

❖ Begin breaking the solution down into smaller steps.

❖ Once you have chosen the best solution the last 5 steps of the Problem Solving Method are the same as the steps in Goal Setting.

Problem Solving Exercise (Example)

Problem – My room is so messy! I'm so busy; it's hard to find time to keep it clean, and I can't find my things when I need them.

Solutions – Clean it once a week, spend 10 minutes daily cleaning, hire a maid, or re-organize.

Best Solution – Re-Organize

Now apply the remaining steps (4-7):

4. Detailed Plan	5. Person responsible	6. Deadline	7. Re-valuate
Buy Containers to separate items	Me	Within 2 weeks	Done
Get rid of things I no longer need	Me	Next weekend	In the process
Put things in their place as I use them	Me	Beginning today	Getting in the habit

Going great! I am now enjoying my extra space and the time I save by knowing where to find my things!

Begin a list of challenges you are facing in reaching your goals. Pick one and apply the steps of problem solving using the forms in the back of this book.

_____

_____

_____

_____

_____

_____

_____

_____

_____

_____

You now have two valuable tools in your toolbox to help you on your path.

❖ *Goal Setting*

❖ *Problem Solving*

It's now time to add a third tool to get you started well on your way to accomplishing your goals.   Read on to learn more about a simple decision making method.

Personal Notes

Personal Notes

_____

_____

_____

_____

_____

_____

_____

_____

_____

_____

_____

_____

_____

_____

_____

_____

_____

Decision Making

Do you ever have a difficult time making a decision? Do you second guess whether or not the decision you made is the best decision for you?

The following method is a variation of the Ben Franklin method and can help you gain confidence that the decisions you make are the right ones for you.

1. What is the decision to be made? Write it down.

2. Make a line down the middle of your paper. On each half of the paper, you will make 2 columns.

3. Label the columns on each side: Pros & Cons.

4. On one side, list the pros & cons of decision option #1.

5. On the other side, list the pros & cons of decision option #2.

6. Look at your lists.

Typically, the right answer is staring you in the face. You may notice that one list is much longer than the other. Or, it may be apparent that some of the cons on one list may be more serious in nature, making that decision unacceptable.

The answer is usually obvious.

<u>Decision Making Exercise (example)</u>

Option #1   Option #2

<u>Should I buy new car?</u>   <u>Should I keep old car?</u>

Pros	Cons	Pros	Cons
Less repair expense	Car Payment	No Payment	Repair expense
Can get different model			Not reliable
Dependable			Not enough room for family
New car smell			

Now review the lists. The decision may vary depending upon your own situation when making this decision. If finances are not a concern, looks like the new car wins! If the payment would create a financial burden, you might want to opt for keeping the older model for a while longer.

You now have three valuable tools in your toolbox you can begin to use immediately.

❖ *Goal Setting*

❖ *Problem Solving*

❖ *Decision Making Method*

Begin a list of decisions you are facing. Pick one and apply the decision method using the forms in the back of this book.

_____

_____

_____

_____

_____

_____

_____

_____

_____

_____

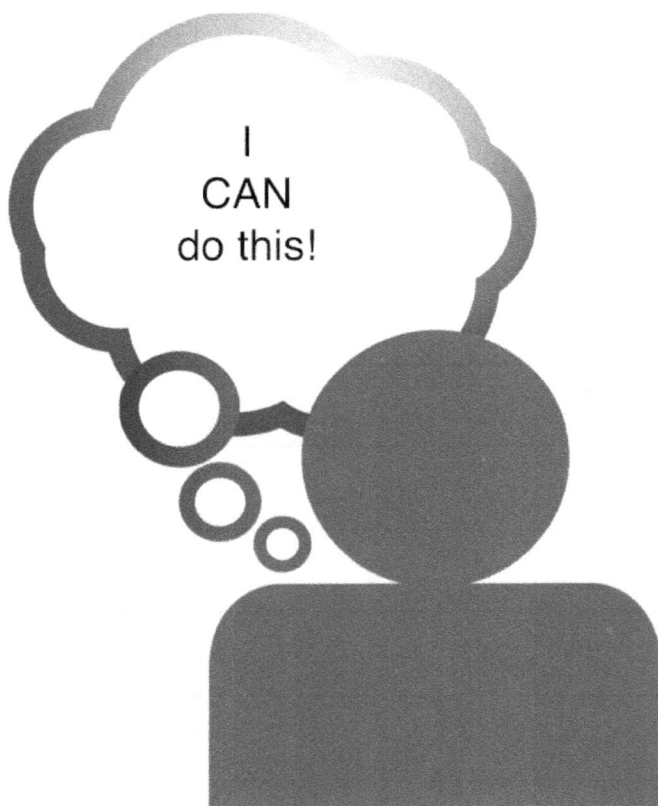

Congratulations on reading and learning these skills. Now apply them to your daily life and track your progress as you travel on your path!

Personal Notes

Personal Notes

_____

_____

_____

_____

_____

_____

_____

_____

_____

_____

_____

_____

_____

_____

_____

_____

_____

_____

Feel better mentally and physically.

Following is a potpourri of tips on how to live a happier, more fulfilled life. As you read, select a few that you feel would make the biggest difference in your life and write them down. Then under each topic write specifics on how you will incorporate them into your daily or weekly routine. Take time on a weekly basis to reflect on any successes you experienced. You may want to begin your own personal journal.

Be thankful, regardless of the answer you receive.

It's easy to be thankful when something we have asked for has been given to us. Have you ever had the experience that you prayed for something that you thought you really needed only to find out later that *not* getting what you asked for was actually a gift? *Did you take the time to give thanks for what you "did not receive?"*

A year or two ago, I began buying lottery tickets hoping to win millions of dollars. When I prayed I would explain to God how "If only I could win the lottery," I could help others that were in need through charity work, and how I could spontaneously help strangers that came across my path. Leaving it to God to determine whether or not I would pick the lucky numbers, I would then wait for the results. I would proceed to buy a ticket each week. Each time I bought a ticket," I had a feeling of ...anxiety of some sort. When the numbers were drawn and I learned I was not a winner, part of me, of course, was disappointed that I was not a winner. The other part of me was somewhat relieved. I would often tell my husband, Don, "You know, I don't think I would really want to WIN millions." My gut instinct told me that it would not bring me the fulfillment that I would get from earning the money through hard work. I knew that winning the lottery was not in my destiny, but that something else bigger and better was. I quit buying lottery tickets and am relying on prayer and asking for guidance to show me the direction I am supposed to take. *Be thankful for unanswered prayers as you continue to ask for guidance.*

Be patient, time will tell ...the adventure is not over yet.

Forgive yourself

There have been many times in my life when I have asked for forgiveness but still felt burdened. I have asked for forgiveness for many things from small to large, that if I had to do over again, I would do differently. One day, while reading the Bible (one of my goals for this year), something that stood out to me was about forgiving yourself. I'm sure I learned that somewhere along the way, but somehow it didn't sink in. I feel that I have been good about forgiving others, but what I learned was I also needed to be better about forgiving myself. I have always been my own worst critic, and others have heard me say, "I am much harder on myself, than anyone else could ever be." *I now know and can have comfort in knowing that once I ask for forgiveness, it is done. I can let it go and focus on the lesson I learned from the situation and how I can use that experience to make me a better person and possibly use that knowledge to help someone else. Forgive yourself. Accept your forgiveness.*

Begin a list of things you want to ask for forgiveness and let it go. Then, think about what you learned from the situation and how it has made you a better person today.

_____

_____

_____

_____

_____

_____

_____

_____

_____

_____

_____

Forgive Others

If you want to be forgiven, you must forgive others first. Are there people in your life that you feel you cannot forgive? How is it affecting you? Is it causing you anxiety? Have you tried to view the situation from the other person's viewpoint?

Sometimes we are guilty of judging the person instead of the circumstances that led to the situation between the two of us.

Wouldn't it be easier to forgive and then move forward?

Forgive without conditions; you will feel better physically and emotionally.

Do it for yourself.   Make a list of those you need to forgive. Focus on the situation, not the person.   Mark them off one at a time as you forgive them.

_____

_____

_____

_____

_____

_____

_____

_____

_____

_____

Make Restitution

Make restitution to the people in your life that you have wronged.   Can you think of anyone that you owe an apology or someone that you mistreated or wronged in some way? Sometimes the other person may not even be aware of how something you said or did affected them in a negative way. Carrying this burden can keep you from experiencing true JOY in your life. You can change it today and make a difference. Begin by making a list of people to whom you owe an apology.   Start there and work your way up. People will have a new respect for you. *The reward for you will be in the comfort and relief you will feel when you can then let it go.*

I want to apologize for the following situations.

_____

_____

_____

_____

_____

_____

_____

_____

_____

_____

_____

Stay in Touch

Keep communication open. A sure way to have regrets is to cut off communication. Someday, it may be too late. If you make attempts toward resolution, even though it is never resolved, you can sleep at night knowing you did your part. The first thing to learn about communication, and probably the most important thing to remember, is to LISTEN first. Take time to LISTEN to the other person. *We all do a fantastic job of talking. Do you offer uninterrupted listening to others?*

Try not to judge others.

Your first impression of a person may be when they are at their worst. *Always remember that you are only getting a glimpse of the true person. Give them the benefit of the doubt and look for the good in them.*

Learn to be less judgmental. My life experience has proven that many times what I criticize others for, I, myself, am guilty of doing. Think about it. The next time you are judging someone, think about yourself and your own life experiences. Are you guilty of the same thing?

Practice what you preach. Set an example. You will earn credibility among your peers.

Help someone without expecting anything in return.

Listen without giving advice.

Wake up each morning asking yourself, "What can I do today to have a positive influence on those around me?" And then do it.

Build people up, instead of putting them down. Support their strengths. Don't focus on their weaknesses. Try thinking of 3 positive attributes for every negative.

"Teach to fish." Help people help themselves. Start by teaching them the steps of goal setting and problem solving.

Think of ways that you can bring JOY to others through your profession. And then put them into action.

Think of ways how you personally can bring JOY to the people with whom you work.

Do one good deed per day. It may be something as simple as picking up trash off the side of the road. At the end of the year, you will have performed 365 deeds. Others may be inspired by your efforts and do the same thing!

Nurture someone in need. For example, take someone to the grocery store, clean their house, prepare a meal, check in on them periodically, or just spend time with them and **listen** to what they have to say.

Help a stranger without expecting anything in return.

Try to spontaneously help others in need when a situation presents itself. For example, I was on a business trip and went to the mall to unwind. There was a young man carrying a heavy load of boxes and attempting to get on the escalator. I walked over and helped him carry the boxes. He very much appreciated my help and said, "I was wondering how I was going to do this". He appreciated my help, but the reward was mine. It made my day!

Focus on good habits you want to create, as well as bad habits you need to change.

Are you involved in making the world a better place? Start by writing down one thing that you can do, starting tomorrow, and then grow from there.

You are not always in charge of the situation you find yourself in, but you are in control of your response.

Stay humble. Things can change in an instant.

Do some "soul searching" and ask yourself: "What are my true motives behind what it is I am about to do?"

Be generous with your time.

Spend your time and energy on what YOU can do better, not on other people's weaknesses.

Be aware and recognize when you get answers to your prayers. Write them down if needed. You will find this amazing if you try it. When you pray for something, you will be amazed at how many of your prayers are being answered that you sometimes take for granted. When you ask for things as simple as finding your car keys to what career path you need to take, always say *thank you* in advance.

Pray for wisdom and guidance each day. Just ask God to give you enough wisdom to make the decisions that are right for you.

Learn something new every day.

Share your knowledge.

Surround yourself with people who have strengths other than yours. Learn from them.

Find a mentor. Find someone you respect that is on the same path that you would like to take for your life. Learn from them.

Model those you respect and that are working for the greater good.

Never lose your enthusiasm. It is easier to be successful at something if you are excited about doing it.

Try to discover what you can do for others without thinking about what they can do for you in return. The rewards will come when you least expect it.

Be thankful for the bad times; there is a lesson to be learned. You will never know if there would have been unforeseen negative consequences if it had happened the way you had planned.

Appreciate those who are different from you.

They can have much to offer you. We all come from different walks of life. We have a wide variety of cultures, lifestyles, and many different life experiences. I find it very interesting to meet others who are different from me. I know that there is something to be learned from that person. Sometimes we judge others for how they are without knowing their life experiences that have shaped the person that we see. *Listen to other people's stories that are unique in your eyes. (Chances are they are thinking YOU are unique.) You will find that it opens a whole new world of understanding and will lead to an appreciation of people that are different from you.*

Remember the Power of Positive Thinking to Lower Stress, Increase Happiness.

Try the following tips.

The power of positive thinking has strengthened my spiritual life. Addressing my fears head on has helped me let go of being afraid of what "might" happen. I put my faith in accomplishing my goals and know that I am being guided. I truly feel that there is a plan for me, and that through prayer and hard work, I will stay on the right path.

Get outside. Walk in the woods, down the street, sit out in the sunshine, breathe fresh air, swim, walk, jog, or lay on the ground.

Never let a day go by without counting your blessings. If you are breathing, you have blessings to count.

Give thanks and appreciation for everything in your life.

Create an atmosphere that is open for communication with your family.

Take time to reflect at the end of the day on the positive things in your life.

Turn off news at the beginning and end of each day. Limit the amount of energy you spend on listening to negative news.

For the first few minutes when you get home from work or school focus on something positive. Make an effort to keep the first 10 minutes of conversation positive; it will set the mood for the evening.

When telling about your day, share the positive. Share the negative only when necessary. You will be amazed at how much better you (and those around you) will feel.

Be willing to let go of past history.

Develop a new belief system where anything is possible – if you are willing to work hard and pray for guidance. Make your dreams come true!

Ask yourself when shopping, will this make a difference in my life in a positive way...Do I really need this? Would I be better served by putting this money in a savings account?
I have learned to ask myself, "Do I need this, or do I want this?"

Think positive about your job situation or begin taking steps to make a change. Work toward creating a positive environment for yourself and others.

Look at what you are doing well, then how can you do it better.

*L*ook at what is NOT going well. Apply the steps of problem solving that you learned earlier to the situation. Re-evaluate what changes you need to make.

*F*ind ways to make a difference in other people's lives through your work. Think about how you can help them, not how they can help you. The rewards will follow.

Lower Stress

It's amazing how positive thinking can lower stress and give you a brighter outlook on life. We have all heard you become what you think about. It is a valid point. Try it. Every time you find yourself thinking negative thoughts, stop and focus on something positive. Continue to do this until you begin to change your habits and your thought patterns. You will find yourself moving toward what you focus on.

Find a balance between work, personal, family, and spiritual needs.

If you need help in finding a balance, try this exercise. Write down under each of the 4 topics what you can do in that category to help create the balance you desire. Then, apply the steps of goal setting to each topic. Use the chart on the following page.

Work-Career	Personal goals
Family	Spiritual

Never let your fears keep you from accomplishing your dreams.

For many years, a fear of flying caused me a great deal of anxiety for days prior to any time I was scheduled to fly. The challenge was that my job involved travel and flying to my clients' offices, sometimes on a weekly basis. I knew I had to address my fears to continue on my career path.

I decided to use the decision making process
mentioned earlier in this book to make a
decision on how to proceed. I listed the pros
and cons of continuing with my work and
flying, and then I listed the pros and cons of
changing careers and choosing a path that did
not involve travel. Through this method I was
able to determine that the benefits of my work
outweighed my fear of flying. I began to realize
that my work was "part of the plan" for my life,
which allowed me to trust that I was on the right
path. I prayed that if this is what was meant for
me, I would overcome my fear of flying, and I
did.

Whew... It feels good to have support.

Don't be anxious or worry, present your worries to God and let him handle them for you. Then let them go.

Live your life in a way that you would look forward to seeing it played back before you in front of your family and friends.

I'm ready to
get started!

$\mathcal{M}$y hope is that you have gained several insights from this book that you can apply to your daily life that will help you along your chosen path....

Always Remember...

The Final Step

Say your prayers and ask for guidance

Top 10 personal insights gained from this book

1.

2.

3.

4.

5.

6.

7.

8.

9.

10.

Things I've chosen to apply to my daily life

1.

2.

3.

4.

5.

6.

7.

8.

9.

10.

<u>Goal Setting Theory</u>

1. Write your goal:

_____

_____

Now apply the remaining steps (2-5):

2. Detailed Plan	3. Person responsible	4. Deadline	5. Re-valuate

6 (Final Step) Ask for guidance- are you on the right track? (Key to my own personal success.)

1. Write your goal:

_____

_____

Now apply the remaining steps (2-5):

2. Detailed Plan	3. Person responsible	4. Deadline	5. Re-valuate

6 (Final Step) Ask for guidance- are you on the right track? (Key to my own personal success.)

1. Write your goal:

_____

_____

Now apply the remaining steps (2-5):

2. Detailed Plan	3. Person responsible	4. Deadline	5. Re-valuate

6 (Final Step) Ask for guidance- are you on the right track? (Key to my own personal success.)

1. Write your goal:

_____

_____

Now apply the remaining steps (2-5):

2. Detailed Plan	3. Person responsible	4. Deadline	5. Re-valuate

6 (Final Step) Ask for guidance- are you on the right track? (Key to my own personal success.)

1. Write your goal:

_____

_____

Now apply the remaining steps (2-5):

2. Detailed Plan	3. Person responsible	4. Deadline	5. Re-valuate

6 (Final Step) Ask for guidance- are you on the right track? (Key to my own personal success.)

1. Write your goal:

_____

_____

Now apply the remaining steps (2-5):

2. Detailed Plan	3. Person responsible	4. Deadline	5. Re-valuate

6 (Final Step) Ask for guidance- are you on the right track? (Key to my own personal success.)

1. Write your goal:

_____

_____

Now apply the remaining steps (2-5):

2. Detailed Plan	3. Person responsible	4. Deadline	5. Re-valuate

6 (Final Step) Ask for guidance- are you on the right track? (Key to my own personal success.)

1. Write your goal:

_____

_____

Now apply the remaining steps (2-5):

2. Detailed Plan	3. Person responsible	4. Deadline	5. Re-valuate

6 (Final Step) Ask for guidance- are you on the right track? (Key to my own personal success.)

<u>Problem Solving</u>

Problem_____

_____

Solutions_____

_____

Best Solution

_____

_____

Now apply the remaining steps (4-7):

4. Detailed Plan	5. Person responsible	6. Deadline	7. Re-valuate

<u>Problem Solving</u>

Problem_____

_____

Solutions_____

_____

Best Solution

_____

_____

Now apply the remaining steps (4-7):

4. Detailed Plan	5. Person responsible	6. Deadline	7. Re-valuate

<u>Problem Solving</u>

Problem_____

_____

Solutions_____

_____

Best Solution

_____

_____

Now apply the remaining steps (4-7):

4. Detailed Plan	5. Person responsible	6. Deadline	7. Re-valuate

Problem Solving

Problem_____

_____

Solutions_____

_____

Best Solution

_____

_____

Now apply the remaining steps (4-7):

4. Detailed Plan	5. Person responsible	6. Deadline	7. Re-valuate

<u>Problem Solving</u>

Problem_____

_____

Solutions_____

_____

Best Solution

_____

_____

Now apply the remaining steps (4-7):

4. Detailed Plan	5. Person responsible	6. Deadline	7. Re-valuate

<u>Problem Solving</u>

Problem_____

_____

Solutions_____

_____

Best Solution

_____

_____

Now apply the remaining steps (4-7):

4. Detailed Plan	5. Person responsible	6. Deadline	7. Re-valuate

Problem Solving

Problem_____

_____

Solutions_____

_____

Best Solution

_____

_____

Now apply the remaining steps (4-7):

4. Detailed Plan	5. Person responsible	6. Deadline	7. Re-valuate

Problem Solving

Problem_____

_____

Solutions_____

_____

Best Solution

_____

_____

Now apply the remaining steps (4-7):

4. Detailed Plan	5. Person responsible	6. Deadline	7. Re-valuate

Decision Making Exercise

Option #1   **Option #2**

_____   _____

_____   _____

Pros	Cons	Pros	Cons

Is your answer obvious? Which list is longer? Are any of the "cons" unacceptable, therefore, making your decision clear?

Decision Making Exercise

Option #1   **Option #2**

_____   _____

_____   _____

Pros	Cons	Pros	Cons

Decision Making Exercise

Option #1   **Option #2**

_____   _____

_____   _____

Pros	Cons	Pros	Cons

<u>Decision Making Exercise</u>

Option #1   **Option #2**

_____   _____

_____   _____

Pros	Cons	Pros	Cons

<u>Decision Making Exercise</u>

Option #1   **Option #2**

_____   _____

_____   _____

Pros	Cons	Pros	Cons

<u>Decision Making Exercise</u>

Option #1   **Option #2**

_____   _____

_____   _____

Pros	Cons	Pros	Cons

Decision Making Exercise

Option #1   **Option #2**

_____   _____

_____   _____

Pros	Cons	Pros	Cons

<u>Decision Making Exercise</u>

Option #1   **Option #2**

_____   _____

_____   _____

Pros	Cons	Pros	Cons

Personal Notes

Personal Notes

_____

_____

_____

_____

_____

_____

_____

_____

_____

_____

_____

_____

_____

_____

_____

_____

_____

About the Author

Judy Risner has worked in the dental industry the majority of her career and is now working as an independent consultant to help others realize their true potential and reach their goals. She is owner of Judy Risner Consulting, LLC and resides with her family in Oklahoma.

Judy is also owner of I Wish I Would Have Thought of That, LLC, dba MY IDEA CAN.com. The mission of this website based business is to help others realize their dreams by providing information, support, helpful tips and success stories shared by others who have paved the way. The website is: www.myideacan.com

Please feel free to contact Judy at

judy@judyrisner.com

www.judyrisner.com

P. O. Box 425

Davis, OK 73030

Thank you for reading this book. I am truly honored. If you have benefited from the time you spent, please tell others. The referral of your family and friends would be my highest compliment.

I welcome any comments, suggestions or testimonials you would like to share. Kindly send to:

Email: judy@judyrisner.com

I would like to personally invite you to also share your success stories at my website below. Feel free to include a personal photo.

www.myideacan.com

www.ingramcontent.com/pod-product-compliance
Lightning Source LLC
Chambersburg PA
CBHW070531030426
42337CB00016B/2175